words from a wanderer.
a poetry collection by laraya billups

author's note.

This book is a compilation of poems written over five years. Those five years have been filled with pain, love, heartbreak, but mostly self-discovery. These poems reflect the beauty of discovering myself in all my authenticity, and I hope it encourages you to discover what makes you beautiful, strong, and at times, a work in progress. Life is all about what we learn, unlearn, and relearn about ourselves and others. I hope you see beauty in your process.

To whoever is reading, It was not by chance that you picked up this book. I wanted to tell you that you have a purpose in life. You are created for a reason — to discover the hidden beauty of yourself.

the wanderer.

fluidity.

the language I speak is spontaneity,

dwelling beyond the confines of everyone's expectations.

I am never still,

I feel a massive wind whisking me off my feet at all times.

I embrace exploration.

freedom is my country.

welcome to my homeland,

where nomads are misunderstood yet necessary.

wanderers give birth to thoughts bound

by closed spirits.

I'm sorry you can't fathom my dialect,

but don't expect me to be silenced by your insecurity.

traveler.

wondering where I've been?

so have I.

my raft at sea finally touches the shore,

but part of me remains drifting.

I wade in the water waiting for a rescue.

I push myself away from the shore with a stroke of my hand.

the mainland is a place of certainty,

of belonging,

and I've always been a castaway.

lately, I'm in search of a home,

and the sea has become my shelter.

necessity.

I wish I was as forgiving

as the plants who pardon the sun for its abandonment.

the leaves cry under the weight of a million raindrops

only to rise

taller

when the sun returns

maybe it is not a punishment

but a necessity.

blood trait.

my sister gazes at night stars.
she finds the quests of ancient warriors.
she breathes in the fantasies of Galileo,
reading the sky like a book with no end.
she points at Orion's belt,
his bow in his hand.
she reminds me of her strength.
my mom views rainbows as promises,
taking photos before
the message melts into the stratosphere.
she tells me God would never destroy this world with water
again.
I always wonder how I flow with the stream,
how I exist in one place
yet remain floating elsewhere.
now I realize
wandering has always been a blood trait.

loose leaf.

I learned how to fold my pain

into fourths,

stashing it in my back pocket and smiling

as if it doesn't exist.

I open it when I'm alone,

caught in the creases of my anxiety.

it's a pattern,

folding and unfolding,

broken then unbroken.

I'm still learning how to throw it away.

drowning.

I'm trying to breathe.
you shoved my head underwater
and as I writhe under the waves,
I find numbness in the sorrow
guzzling down the salty grains of the ocean
until I'm choking on every lie you ever told me.
it tastes like every lie I tell myself.
tell me what I did to deserve to drown.
tell me how to survive losing myself, and which
direction to swim to where my old self floats.

voice.

my voice is timid.

she's never gotten a chance to speak,

to be heard.

so forgive her nervousness.

this is her first time,

her first burst of bravery after living in the shadows.

it's overwhelming to know people are listening,

yet it is endearing to know she exists.

flight.

eyes wide open.

hands outstretched.

take a leap of faith.

tie a harness to my chest,

I'm learning to fall without the promise of success,

but with a hope of finding refuge.

masterpiece.

I allowed you to hold my paintbrush,

to color my canvas

according to your standards of beauty and character.

my painting is theft,

molded into the mosaic you desired,

and it's my mistake for giving you that power.

it's my mistake for never speaking up.

I'm taking my paintbrush back,

my artistic integrity,

my vibrant hues.

from now on, you have no say in how I sculpt my masterpiece.

poet.

poetry is a glimpse into the soul.

a prayer that cries out to be heard,

a dream everyone relates to dreaming.

poetry is the way we writers cope.

twisting words to fit our emotional state,

and exposure that's never easy to feel.

it's especially hard when I don't know what to feel at all.

I write in grand metaphors and similes,

a master of repetition and verse,

but sometimes I aim to be simple.

sometimes I just want to say I'm hurting,

and I want people to hear me cry.

introspection.

a cloudy mind begs for introspection.
I assumed I was on the right path,
but I feel like I'm walking without a map to a discreet destination.
I wish I knew the secret,
the secret of opening up to God without trust issues.
what do I do when He tells me to sit in uncertainty?
when it seems like everyone else has it together except for me?
I'm in flight like a dove in the wind,
just looking for a place to land,
to show me what it's like to love life in every season.
the tears, the laughter,
even the frustration.
when I'm still ignorant to life lessons,
no matter how many times I've taken the class.
maybe there will always be a cloudy region of my mind,
a region I refuse to linger in because I would lose all hope.
I must keep myself afloat.
keep my hands out in case I lose my grip on the oars of my boat.
keep my mouth open to speak to God

even when nobody else falls to their knees.

we're all on this mission to settle on the shore,

never needing more.

I'm blessed with the opportunity to never live in a state of lack,

not within myself anymore.

lies.

at the end of the day, there is me,

no longer distracted by the demands of living anymore.

alone in my thoughts,

I crawl into bed with the same words echoing in my head.

"you are a mistake"

"you are unworthy"

"you are not meant to be here"

I fall asleep to this playlist every night.

it's a learning process to

always think positively

but you have to.

never fall asleep to a replay of self-hatred.

at the end of the night, the demons come alive.

protect yourself from their lies.

explorer.

there's a place
made just for me
a beautiful island
only me,
the beach
and the sea
unfazed by the whereabouts of the mainland
I could not stay.
in that world,
I could not conform.
I tried the best I could
always failing
never succeeding
my shortcomings on display.
I went to the island for solace
escape from the aches and pain
the perfect medication
slipping into a world
that knows not your name.
life is merely an illusion of boundlessness
and I long for satisfaction.
I found a place made just for me.

now

it's only me

the beach

and the sea

on the island

where a soul can be free.

time.

time was overrated until it vanished,

neglecting to ask permission to stay or leave.

time was never patient,

always ready to commence without anyone else's input.

time only hoped we would forgive its transgressions

against our own will.

sometimes I wonder what time is personified,

someone acknowledged yet always defied,

dwindling from years to mere minutes to make life decisions.

tender.

I know I am

more tender than hard-hearted,

more beauty than ashes.

I'm learning to appreciate the moments of hate

that taught me how to love.

strength.

strength is not a measure of retaliation.

strength is not a measure of denying pain.

strength is acknowledging pain,

wrapping my arms around the wound,

and choosing to smile.

becoming.

my craft is my life.
I water my mind throughout the day,
I pray for my words at night.
I want you to hear me in the morning,
sprouting from the roots of my heart,
blooming into the woman I hoped I would be,
who would be a blessing to others.
I pray that you grow.
I pray you sow the seeds to begin your transformation into an elegant flower,
poised and brilliant.
radiant and willing.
willing to harness your beauty to catch the eye of a hurting stranger,
and bestowing your love upon them.

weight.

I can carry the weight of the world,

the hopes of every living being

and every thought of distress.

I overdose on empathy,
somehow always finding a fix.
someone save me from this addiction,
this voice that tells me
every fault is mine to carry,
my sins to atone for
even though my heart knows the world
is not mine to align,
not mine to correct,
not mine to interject.
I live as a barely human passenger,
only a compilation of others,
carrying everyone's cracked smile.

journey.

these words are the only luggage my soul carries,

scribbled into paper napkins and outstretched palms.

I live a wanderer's life,

a foreigner in my own mind,

discovering uncharted territory inside myself that I never knew existed,

that I'm excited to explore.

I'm convinced that loving me is not an impossible task.

it's an incredible journey.

uncertainty.

words evade my thoughts

until I am only feeling,

feeling through the intensity of my own emotion.

I'm trying to name how it feels to be alive,

and all that existing entails.

the strength to discover through unfamiliarity.

the purity to understand

while being understood.

know that I am not rushing for sunshine,

for the sun rises when she is ready to be seen.

these days, I am okay with skies of gray,

okay with uncertainty.

urgency.

meet me in the middle.

find me in distant dimensions,

open-air,

unfiltered, and unashamed.

nothing but elaborate plans to my name.

help me to lose my dependence on control.

a detailed planner with an expansive imagination,

I get caught up in fantasy too much,

never in reality too long.

bring me back to an earthly level.

teach my vessel that it is alright to live in the moment

without knowing what this moment means.

why do I always feel an urgency?

to have it all written before I reach 25,

to find a way to not be lonely at night by 29?

human.

exhaustion greets me even when I'm wide awake.
I recognize where I am,
but I always reach for a compass.
my mouth utters apologies when I'm not at fault.
loneliness consumes me,
but sometimes, I savor seclusion more than another's presence.
everything I desire, I cease to fight for,
and everything I never asked for,
I struggle to release.
it's strange that nobody truly understands humanity,
yet each day, we operate in human emotion.
but maybe there's a certain beauty to being so imperfect,
a certain innocence and unity,
that we're all searching when we've already been found.

blossom.

deep roots.

uprooted by the storms.

swallowed by the river.

I thought I planted deep enough

where you couldn't see rotten skin.

I teach everyone how to dig,

yet I left no room to blossom.

performance.

I equate gratitude to an endless sky.

I consider how most days,

the sun claims the stage, and as the audience,

we gaze in awe of the production.

we give standing ovations at the ending scene.

but on days when the sun must be the understudy to the clouds,

when the climax erupts,

I still find strength in the sun's performance.

even without a clear presence,

I know the difference between night and day,

and I know she'll rise again.

flame.

I tried to water myself down for you,

but it was you who couldn't handle my flame.

unconscious.

lately, I've been trying to sleep it away,

but I always wake up to the thoughts in my head

arguing over which one will consume my day.

stuck between fear and faith,

peace or anxiety,

and I feel like I'm lacking a choice.

I know God is a healer,

but I retract from Him due to my insecurity of proximity.

I attempt to find my healing subconsciously.

let me sleep one more minute,

let me have another moment to pretend like everything is

alright when I'm falling apart and just watching it happen.

I had a discussion,

a heart-to-heart with my spirit that begs for change,

but first I have to believe it can happen for me.

that the love I give extends to my being as well as others,

that I am forgiven even though I haven't lived outside of my

pain.

I cannot be a bystander any longer.

it is never too late to be free.

it is never too late to forgive me,

and I've never had to forgive myself for closing the door,

for wrapping myself in the warm covers,
 and closing my eyes to forget the discontent.
let me sleep again,
because everything feels better when I'm unconscious,
but it's time to wake up.

foundation.

my scars won't allow me to build the same structure twice.
shards of glass remain in my skin from trying to reassemble
what was broken,
but they will never reflect like before.
foundations must collapse before something beautiful
emerges,
this soul hasn't been a home for years,
so I'm making a new blueprint.
I'm not trying to prove anyone wrong anymore.
there's a greater use for these bricks.
I take a photo to capture
the growth frame by frame,
knowing there is beauty ahead.

breathe.

I pray to inhale new breath
filling my punctured lungs with air
that won't escape.
inflate my will to exist for a purpose.
breathing is the greatest miracle,
reviving what begs for resurrection.
breathing isn't appreciated
until it is crucial.
I cling to what's left of my breath,
finding the strength to inhale
and release.

thirst.

an empty church parking lot
and a playlist entitled escape,
but I'm unsure how I'll flee this time.
I used to love it here,
back when life made more sense.
now love is just as foreign as my reflection,
rugged terrain against my skin.
I blame it on the stress.
an empty church parking lot
and the grass is still cut
and the cross still stands.
I find comfort in how the cross sustains,
even when I'm not there to witness it each day.
it has no sash.
I believe it's supposed to be white after easter.
indicative of a resurrection.
who will rise from the ashes of my soul?
an empty church parking lot
except for one misguided girl,
a woman at the well unnamed seeking water.
I wonder if she ever remembered what thirst felt like,
how satisfied she became at that moment.

back when the parking lot was full.

now I thirst for cars to pull up

to remind me what it means to be filled.

vagabond.

I have been a wanderer for too long.
walking alone through every desert and wet season,
then you came along and offered shelter.
maybe I forgot what it means to be lonely,
to want someone enduring the weather with me.
yes, I say I love you,
but I also love the leaving,
the adventure,
the idea that someone sees the sunset as the end
and I envision a beginning.
I'll always be floating between continents.
I chase after love,
certain that I'll watch it fade with the current.
wanderers don't find passion.
people risk leaving their hearts in my hands.
wanderers don't find stability.
nobody stays too long.
wanderers don't find a home.
I am only a shelter for vagabonds.

shiver.

early morning wishes to be in your arms,
but you've kept me far from your vulnerability,
leaving me to wonder
if you remain warm and susceptible to love.
I walk into your snowstorms without a coat,
without a covering,
hoping you would see the measures I would take to
thaw your heart.
I'm in awe of how distant you can be.
you offer minimal warmth,
you leave me without your body heat.
can't you see I'm still freezing,
or is this your punishment for me?
my early morning thoughts transform
into early morning dreams,
of needs I never knew I desired,
of wounds I already thought had healed.

real.

forgive me if I think of us more often

than I should.

I just wonder

how you could give up on me

when my love was too precious.

when I offered you the world,

you still decided to search

for something real.

construction.
this foundation has known faults since its conception
but still stands firm.
these cracks have filled with laughter,
plastered within the walls.
my spirit is a house, but not a home.
buildings must collapse before something beautiful emerges,
and what I've been building after the storm has taken more time
than what was initially there.
construction has decided on its time frame.
right now, it's nowhere in the foreseeable future.
don't ask me when I'm having my housewarming,
or when I'll plant the flowers.
I'm still dealing with the aftermath of neighbors who vandalized my space,
so don't ask me when I'll reopen.
I can't build the same thing twice.
there's a greater use for these bricks,
I'm pulling up my sleeves because I'm done with breaking promises to myself,
and I apologize for the several blueprints I've thrown away,

the drafted floor plans of the places I thought I could never enter.

I apologize that I never gave myself the confidence to be a homeowner,

to see my outside as gorgeous and my inside as purity.

my future home changes the narrative.

my home has more than four walls with a jacked-up white picket fence.

my home is a lamp unto my feet and light unto my path.

my home is decorated in my design.

all the beautiful things are built with time.

little by little, a home is forged from the ashes.

bankrupt.

I give my heart to hands foreign to my form of love.

I withdraw,

not because of the investment

but the possibility of a return.

I shouldn't fear wealth as much as bankruptcy,

refusing to believe that you'll exchange

my love for a feeling you find yourself needing in the future.

love is a dangerous purchase,

liable to be laid away at any time.

I guess I'm asking,

is love worth the price?

aiko.

shame on me for changing.
shame on you for staying the same.
rearranging the pieces of our relationship until it resembles art,
we dream that we made it that way,
that the love we constructed was our own doing,
and fate is a four-letter word we both didn't believe in,
but now we're anchored to fate's ship,
drawing us further from individuality.
I'm missing my sense of belonging to myself.
I forgot what freedom means,
so grant me the space to explore it.
I forgot what changing means,
so give me the chance to enjoy it.
like a force, fate grabbed me by the feet,
dragging me into your arms,
and I don't wanna release
but what is love if not letting go?
someday, we'll grow,
and it's up to us to choose
to slip into the crevices of each other's hearts
when we're compatible,

to allow our changing spirits to embrace the same breeze in a different light.

childlike.

I often get mistaken for being younger than I am.
people see me and believe I'm barely in my teens,
yet although I'm all of twenty-two,
sometimes I still feel fifteen.
I'm relearning who I am,
the person I was before I valued the child within me.
a child is unapologetically themselves,
partially because there is nothing else better to be,
but also there are no contingencies.
today I am an astronaut,
but tomorrow I'm planning to reign as queen.
a child knows no limitations,
they only know dreams.
in between Hasbro games and G.I Joe,
our dreams are forced into our toy boxes,
dreading the day where Andy will grow.
childhoods lodged into the four corners of white envelopes
for the means to achieve through credit card schemes.
how much imagination can I apply to a bank account,
to plane tickets to explore?
imagination has been struggling to open closed doors.

I'm fifteen when I realize dreams need a little more power than I can exude,
not just elbow grease but the power to cease the cycles my parents created,
to break unhealthy connections depriving me of creativity.
adulting is not merely running errands,
it's making sure I'm running on full and not on empty,
void of every vision cultivated in my childlike eyes.
if I become myself, maybe I'll stop searching for enough,
and search for more.
I'm all of twenty-two,
and I'm not ashamed to still be a child,
because children know what it means to live.

beauty.

beautiful girl.

attempting to attract eyes.

determined to change minds.

I met you last night,

in a moment of comparison,

you said invisibility is your curse.

beautiful girl.

your concept of beauty lies contingent

on how many people congratulate you on your appearance.

it is not that you're invisible.

I am now realizing

beauty is not in the eye of the beholder,

but in the mind of the beholder.

I believe I am beautiful

therefore I am.

prisoner.

we won't always be prisoners to the cells.

we locked ourselves in,

or others denied us a hearing.

I had time to evaluate my sentence.

in my distance,

I discovered I sentenced myself a long time ago.

I already suggested I was unworthy,

there was no need for the jury to decide.

I won't always be a prisoner of the issues

I couldn't see myself releasing.

realizing my innocence was the first step.

release.

take your time.

relax each muscle in your arms

teach yourself how to let go,

how to let yourself grow.

while the world practices its unison harmony,

you are downbeat,

molding a symphony people learn to love

without a complete orchestra.

only you know your sound.

free of complacency,

consistent with everyone's lack of authenticity.

time has always been on your side,

but it never halts long enough to realize

the minority hums the strongest melodies.

in a few years,

you'll wonder if you were ever carrying your tune.

blooming.

it took me a while to get to this stage,

where I finally know who I am,

and who I was meant to become.

I call this the blooming stage.

I might shed a few petals,

but I always remember

petals grow back more vibrant than they did before.

roots.

I'm back to where it all began,
where I wish I never left.
the arms that never complained about my heavy load.
the legs that carried me where I couldn't take myself.
I ask my soul
when was the moment
it became thirsty,
when the well dried up without any reprieve.
it tells me it lacked the second
I chose not to believe.
when I decided to neglect the past miracles and provide for my own needs,
desperate to fill a need that I could not discern.
the gardener has been good to me,
attended to my every need without asking,
trimmed away the weeds when I couldn't breathe.
when did I start believing that I knew more than the one who planted me?
a seed in the ground
attempting to grow without the gardener
is a seed destined to stay complacent,
unable to grow roots beneath the soil,

tossed around in the wind,

and I'm trying to maintain my footing,

to find a little stability within,

but my efforts are futile

until the gardener plants me again.

image.
I once asked if time would be proud of how I spent it,
choosing not to address that my life has not been well spent.
it's been time left second-guessing,
overestimating, and looking at my image,
unimpressed with what I had seen.
we don't realize how precious our time is
until we're wondering where it's gone.
we are stuck with an image of ourselves we don't recognize,
in a mirror that captures every missed opportunity and misguided mistake.
everyone strives to become the image in their imagination,
the person beyond what their current circumstances can conceive.
I look at my image and ask who she is.
not her mother nor her father but a different breed,
she's deciding between who she has become and who she's meant to be.
I wonder what I hated so much about my image
that I wasted time snuffing out my originality
when I traded everything about me for someone else's misconceptions

when the words hidden in my heart were stripped away from me.

we waste so much time altering our image that we neglect to see the value of the original.

no matter how flawed,

it was still beautiful,

still authentic in its reflection.

.
.
.

mercy.

we give grace to everyone

except for our bodies,

resurrecting others to let ourselves die.

we assume the writing on the wall is the final line

of our final chapter.

I ask myself instead,

what if my greatest failures

are my purest beginnings?

nomad.

this time around,
I'll accept my humanity.
to unclasp my numbing fingers holding onto everything
I cannot change.
forgiveness for the girl left unexpressed.
God blesses the child
who has a strong sense of self,
and the most change started with what has departed,
what has been so difficult to find.
could searching have only made me feel like something was missing?
persistent to present something perfect to be praised,
but I haven't felt like myself in years.
my disconnection causes friction between who I am,
and who I'm praying to be,
feeling too young to be living so old.
so forgive my inconsistency.
for now, I let myself feel what is temporary,
looking forward to what is permanent.
consider this another trip through the pages,
refining another love letter to my resilience,
of the growth I have yet to bloom

moonchild.

this golden child didn't always like the sun.

at times, the sun felt foreign,

the sensation of light tickling my skin.

my reflex is to hide,

seek shelter from the heat.

what could it offer, other than exposure,

everything I assumed I didn't need.

I tend to block what I need the most.

I called myself moonchild because even the stars arrive only by request.

the moon decides to be alone if it desires,

or not to show up at all.

before I belonged to the sun,

I was sure being alone was best.

now I love the warmth,

the way I bask in the sun's rays.

now the light feels like freedom.

twenty.

twenty something.

and I never thought I could be so dependent,

open-hearted to the point where anything could enter,

but nobody told me matters of the heart take time to exit.

I keep reaching into my skin for the neediness poisoning my veins.

twenty something

and I'm always begging people to stay

because I can't ask myself to linger.

the more I stay, the more I see what is struggling to survive.

if I dwell on another, my trauma is not as visible.

twenty something

and I'm still learning how to let go and remind myself that my life is worth living.

my heart is worth protecting.

my limbs do not always have to carry what does not belong to me.

your ink was never meant to bleed onto my story.

twenty something,

and finally, I'm tired of waiting for others to be full before I pour anything into my cup.

I'm seeing what is happening for me,

and it's beautiful,

and it's broken,

and it's imperfect.

but it's mine.

twenty something,

and now I'm ready to say I don't need to use you to avoid myself anymore.

darkness.

I've been thinking about the sunshine,
how it graces the gloom in the world,
caressing my heart in the innocence of the morning.
there's hope that I long to feel each day
because darkness always seems to persist.
I've been told that I can't be surprised by the world anymore,
taken aback by the violence and the cruelty.
I guess I'm more naive,
tied to a dream that the world isn't as evil as it seems
but everyday I'm reminded of reality.
this world will always be self-serving,
desiring their own will over the desperation of another's,
craving the option of feeling vindicated over doing what's right.
I don't claim to be perfect,
but I pray to never become like what I see,
where hatred drives my actions,
greed motivates my desires
and I begin to treat others
as beneath and not equal.
I may not be surprised by the world,
but I am surprised by how beautiful I can be.

golden.

I am property of the sunshine.

illuminating in a gorgeous light.

compassionate and kind.

learning to glow in my own skin.

I am meant to dwell here,

an inhabitant of the sun's beams.

I am infinite.

I am imperfect.

I am meant to be here.

alright.

just keep your head up.

you're gonna be alright.

they saw you cry.

but you're gonna be alright.

they tried to break your spirit,

but you're gonna be alright.

feels like life is crashing,

but you're gonna be alright.

you are covered by God.

you've already been alright.

life knocks us down,

but we're gonna be alright.

don't worry,

you were always meant to be alright.

forgiveness.

I pray you learn the beauty of forgiveness.

not just for yourself, but for others.

cruel people feed on your hate.

starve them with your ability to love.

nostalgia.

it feels strange to say I miss me,

and all that entailed within my personality.

everything that I once loved that molded me.

I'm rediscovering who I was

before I believed that being me was obsolete.

alive.

I have to convince myself

I'm alive.

I interlock my fingers to remind myself of the edges of my skin,

the calloused and the healing.

I must deliberately pull myself out of my thoughts,

the darkest dimensions I create,

to remind myself of reality.

trapped living on contingency.

breathing on dependency.

I reach for the moment when life will not just be for survival,

but living should be an abundant experience.

reminders.

this is just a reminder to myself

to explore,

to never lose the inkling of something greater,

to never get complacent.

I remind myself that my soul needs a breeze to cling to,

a breath to inhale

when I deprive my lungs of air.

I promise to give myself the space to wander,

without a definition

or a time limit,

without another being or another destination.

maybe it's all about the restless travels,

and the woman sent to experience them.

notes.

"Aiko" is after Jhene Aiko's song "Spotless Mind."

"Nomad" features a line from Drake's song "Over" in the 15th line.

acknowledgements.

God,

Thank you for your grace and mercy. Thank you for the divine words you've given me to create this book. I thank you, Lord, that even as I wander through this life, I have never been alone or lost. I simply had to look within myself to be found. Thank you for every lesson I learned that helped develop the poetry and thoughts written inside this book, and I pray that my words could influence someone to keep going.

Thank you to my mom, who has offered unconditional love to me and my sisters every day of our lives. Thank you Mom for the hard work and sacrifices you have made for everything I needed and wanted. Thank you to my sisters for always being there for me and putting up with me for 22 years now.

To my aunts and uncles, each one of you influenced me to live with laughter and grow in Christ. I aspire to make each one of you proud.

To my grandmother who is looking down on me, I pray that you're proud of me as well.

To my best friends, thank you for the laughter. Thank you for the late-night calls and road trips. Thank you for accepting me in every stage of life, helping me to grow. Thank you for supporting this project that was years in the making.

about the author.

Laraya Billups is a college graduate of Bridgewater College with a bachelor's degree in Professional Writing and Communications. She has previously been published in the poetry and short story collection entitled *Delicate Chaos*, and *the Syndrome Mag*. She lives in Toano, Virginia.

www.ingramcontent.com/pod-product-compliance
Lightning Source LLC
LaVergne TN
LVHW021622080426
835510LV00019B/2722